Oct 2020

ENTER THE DOJO!

MARTIAL ARTS FOR KIDS

TAE KWON DO

PHIL CORSO

PowerKiDS
press
New York

Published in 2020 by The Rosen Publishing Group, Inc.
29 East 21st Street, New York, NY 10010

First Edition

Editor: Greg Roza
Book Design: Reann Nye

Photo Credits: Series art Reinhold Leitner/Shutterstock.com; cover Lintao Zhang/Getty Images Sport/Getty Images; pp. 5, 15 didesign021/Shutterstokc.com; p. 6 Top Photo Engineer/Shutterstock.com; p. 7 AFP/Getty Images; p. 9 Paul Archuleta/FilmMagic/Getty Images; p. 10 Dusan Petkovic/Shutterstock.com; p. 11 NurPhoto/Getty Images; p. 12 Jade ThaiCatwalk/Shutterstock.com; p. 13 Drazen Lovric/E+/Getty Images; p. 17 Yamtono_Sardi/iStock/Getty Images Plus/Getty Images; p. 18 Maria Bobrova/Shutterstock.com; p. 19 JUNG YEON-JE/AFP/Getty Images; p. 21 Dusan Petkovic/Shutterstock.com; p. 22 sharpner/Shutterock.com.

Cataloging-in-Publication Data

Names: Corso, Phil.
Title: Tae kwon do / Phil Corso.
Description: New York : PowerKids Press, 2020. | Series: Enter the dojo! martial arts for kids | Includes glossary and index.
Identifiers: ISBN 9781725310223 (pbk.) | ISBN 9781725310247 (library bound) | ISBN 9781725310230 (6 pack)
Subjects: LCSH: Tae kwon do-Juvenile literature.
Classification: LCC GV1114.9 C66 2020 | DDC 796.815'7-dc23

Manufactured in the United States of America

The activities discussed and displayed in this book can cause serious injury when attempted by someone who is untrained in the martial arts. Never try to replicate the techniques in this book without the supervision of a trained martial arts instructor.

CPSIA Compliance Information: Batch #CWPK20. For Further Information contact Rosen Publishing, New York, New York at 1-800-237-9932.

CONTENTS

Knowing Tae Kwon Do

Tae kwon do is many different things. It's an ancient martial art. It's a fighting style used for self-defense. It's an Olympic sport. It's also a **discipline** that goes far beyond just physical skill because its main objective is avoiding **violence**, rather than seeking it.

Tae kwon do started in Korea more than 2,000 years ago as a defense style called "Subak" or "Taekkyon" and was intended to train both the body and mind. "Tae kwon do" loosely means "the way of the foot and fist." The martial art teaches many attacks, but it also teaches ways to calm down fights and keep peace.

Kiai!

Tae kwon do is a national sport in South Korea. The South Korean military uses it as a key piece of its training practices.

Tae kwon do is an ancient fighting style of martial art that draws **athletes** across the globe.

Wall to Mat

The art of tae kwon do began in Korea more than 2,000 years ago and is known as one of the oldest forms of martial art in the world. When it all started, Korea was divided into three kingdoms called Silla, Koguryo and Paekche. Old paintings from that time show people using techniques similar to those used in tae kwon do today.

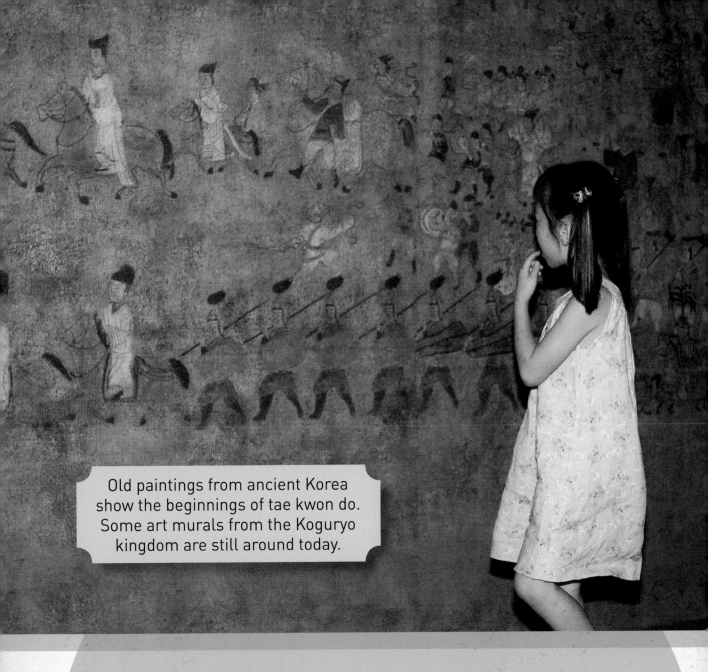

Old paintings from ancient Korea show the beginnings of tae kwon do. Some art murals from the Koguryo kingdom are still around today.

While the Koguryo kingdom first started using the art form, it is said that warriors from the Silla kingdom helped it to grow and spread throughout Korea. Being the smallest of the three kingdoms, it was always under attack.

A League of Its Own

When learning about tae kwon do, some people might wonder how it's different from karate. Both are popular martial arts, and both encourage self-discipline and personal growth. But there are also key differences between the two.

Karate focuses on hand strikes and tae kwon do uses mostly kicking **techniques**, dodges, and blocks using both the hands and feet. The origins of the two art forms are also different. Karate originated in Japan and parts of China, but tae kwon do was founded in Korea. Tae kwon do has been a part of the Olympics since 1988, while Olympic karate was first introduced in 2020.

Kiai!

Tae kwon do has had its fair share of the spotlight in popular Hong Kong and Hollywood action movies starring actors such as Chuck Norris, Jean-Claude Van Damme, and Tony Jaa.

Thai movie star Tony Jaa, shown here, has mastered numerous martial arts. He started with Muay Thai, also called Thai boxing. Jaa has also studied kung fu, judo, and tae kwon do.

Olympic Proportions

While the style of tae kwon do began a long time ago, it did not make its Olympic **debut** as a **demonstration** until the 1988 Seoul Games and later on as an official medal sport during the 2000 Olympic Games in Sydney, Australia. Since then, it has been one of three martial arts featured in the games. The others are judo and katrate.

Kiai!

Tae kwon do clubs often host competitions to attract new students. It has also been a world-class sport for women for many years, generally long before other martial arts.

Tae kwon do is still somewhat new to the Olympic games. By the end of 2008, the sport had more than seven million individuals with black belts. Someone with a black belt has mastered the basics of the martial art.

The art form is practiced in close to 200 countries around the world. In the Olympics, it includes four weight classes each for men and women. Contests are scored by giving one to three points to fighters in single-**elimination** competitions.

Kick It!

You will learn many kinds of kicks throughout your tae kwon do journey while **sparring**, and each one has its own name and style. For example, one basic kick is the axe kick, which is when you raise your leg up high and then bring your heel down on your target. A roundhouse kick is when you twist your hips and use your rear leg to strike your target.

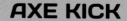

AXE KICK

There are several kicking techniques in tae kwon do and each of them can be learned and practiced using a kicking bag like this one.

There are also more advanced styles for kicking, like the hurricane kick, also known as the tornado kick. You spin your body 360, 540, or 720 degrees and use **momentum** to land a tornado kick.

Train Like a Pro

Training is a key part of mastering the art of tae kwon do. In order to stay sharp and improve your **endurance**, **flexibility**, and strength, there are several techniques you should consider when you enter the dojo, which is a place where martial arts are taught.

Most importantly, stretching should always be a part of anyone's training. It keeps the body healthy and helps avoid injury. But other important training techniques include sparring with another trainee, target-kicking practice, punching techniques, and more.

It is also important to keep a positive frame of mind. Tae kwon do training is about being healthy in the mind as well as the body.

One of the most important parts of training in a martial art is stretching before class.

Around the Waist

The belt system in tae kwon do includes six colors, starting with white for beginners. Students work up through yellow, green, blue, red, and black belts.

White belts indicate "innocence" (or purity) and are reserved for anyone new to tae kwon do. Yellow belts show you have basic knowledge of techniques. Green belt means you are growing as a student. Blue indicates you are doing well in the art. Red stands for danger, meaning you should practice control of your movements. Last, black, as in the opposite of white, stands for growth and a mastery of the form.

Kiai!

Out of all the martial arts, tae kwon do has one of the lowest injury rates. The two most common injuries that fighters might encounter are leg strains and bruises.

The color of your belt tells others just how far along you are in your tae kwon do journey. A black belt shows others that you have mastered the basics of tae kwon do.

Tae Kwon-Pros

If you want to be the best, it helps to learn from the best. Some of the top names in tae kwon do include Hadi Saei Bonehkohal—one of the most successful Iranian athletes in Olympics history—and American Steven López, an Olympic gold medalist. Spanish athlete Joel González won the gold medal in tae kwon do at the 2012 Summer Olympics against South Korean fighter Lee Dae-Hoon.

There are also many women who have become top fighters, including Carmela Hartnett from Australia, Adena Friedman from the United States, and Hwang Kyon-Seon from South Korea, where tae kwon do got its start.

The Modern Art Form

The tae kwon do art form has changed greatly over the centuries. At its beginning, it was mainly a form of self-defense and a military skill. But today, it's treated as a **competitive** sport with the goal of scoring points and showing skill and **precision**.

As the style changed, so did the methods of training. As tae kwon do became more about fun, its methods of practice also changed to focus more on performance, making it one of the most effective styles of unarmed self-defense in the world. This has also increased the number of techniques available to tae kwon do athletes.

Kiai!

In karate, the outfit worn is called a gi. But in tae kwon do, the uniform is a white uniform with a belt tied around the waist called a dobok.

Tae kwon do students spend a lot of time drilling kicking techniques. They use different kinds of pads to train.

21

What Is Success?

If you want to succeed in tae kwon do, you have to put your best foot forward. Going to class regularly is a big part of improving your skills. That could also mean practicing at home with help from an instructor. The best way to learn a new kick or technique is to drill it over and over, whether that's at the dojo with a class, or at home with a punching bag.

Small improvements in tae kwon do will inspire you to continue. As you improve, so will your technique and style. Also, you will likely make lifelong friends in the dojo.

GLOSSARY

athlete: A person who is trained in or good at games and exercises that require skill and strength.

competitive: Having a strong desire to win or be the best at something.

debut: The first appearance.

demonstration: An act of showing someone how something is used or done.

discipline: To train yourself to do something by controlling your behavior.

elimination: The act of removing someone or something.

endurance: The ability to do something difficult for a long time.

flexibility: Capable of bending or stretching without injury.

momentum: The strength or force that something has when it is moving.

precision: Done in a very careful and exact way.

spar: To practice a martial art with another person.

technique: The manner in which physical movements are used for a particular purpose, such as training in a martial art.

violence: The use of force to harm a person or damage property.

INDEX

WEBSITES

Due to the changing nature of Internet links, PowerKids Press has developed an online list of websites related to the subject of this book. This site is updated regularly. Please use this link to access the list: www.powerkidslinks.com/ETD/taekwondo